•••● *BULLETPOINTS* ●•••

TRICERATOPS
AND OTHER PLANT-EATING DINOSAURS

Steve Parker
Consultant: Dr Jim Flegg

Miles Kelly
PUBLISHING

First published in 2003 by Miles Kelly Publishing Ltd
Bardfield Centre, Great Bardfield
Essex, CM7 4SL

Some material in this book first appeared in *1000 Things you should know*

2 4 6 8 10 9 7 5 3 1

Editor: Ruth Boardman

Design: Starry Dog Books

Picture Research: Liberty Newton

Assistant: Carol Danenbergs

Production: Estela Godoy

British Library Cataloguing-in-Publication Data
A catalogue record for this book is available from the British Library

ISBN 1-84236-257-7

Printed in China

www.mileskelly.net
info@mileskelly.net

The publishers would like to thank the following artists who have contributed to this book:
Chris Buzer (Galante Studio), Jim Channell, Brian Delf, Fiametta Dogi (Scientific Illustrations), Chris Forsey,
L R Galante (Galante Studio), Shami Ghale, Alan Hancocks, Steve Kirk, Kevin Maddison, Alan Male (Linden Artists),
Janos Marffy, Gill Platt, Terry Riley, Steve Roberts, Guy Smith (Mainline Design), Sarah Smith, Rudi Vizi,
Christian Webb (Temple Rogers), Steve Weston, Mike White (Temple Rogers)
All other photographs are from: MKP archives; Corbis Professional; Corel Corporation; PhotoDisc

Contents

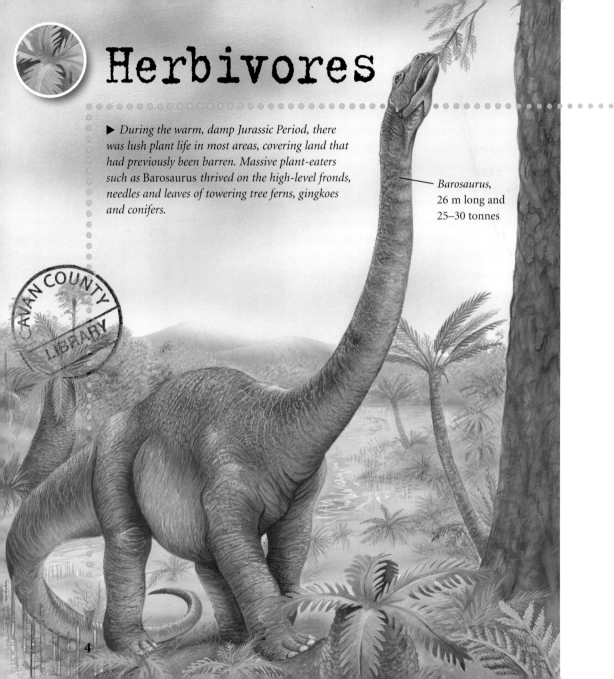

Herbivores

▶ *During the warm, damp Jurassic Period, there was lush plant life in most areas, covering land that had previously been barren. Massive plant-eaters such as* Barosaurus *thrived on the high-level fronds, needles and leaves of towering tree ferns, gingkoes and conifers.*

Barosaurus,
26 m long and
25–30 tonnes

- **Hundreds of kinds of dinosaur** were herbivores, or plant-eaters. As time passed, the plants available for them to eat changed or evolved.

- **Early in the Age of Dinosaurs,** during the Triassic Period, the main plants for dinosaurs to eat were conifer trees, gingkoes, cycads and the smaller seed-ferns, ferns, horsetails and club-mosses.

- **A few cycads** are still found today. They resemble palm trees, with umbrella-like crowns of long green fronds on top of tall, bare, trunk-like stems.

- **In the Triassic Period**, only prosauropod dinosaurs were big enough or had necks long enough to reach tall cycad fronds or gingko leaves.

- **In the Jurassic Period**, tall conifers such as redwoods and 'monkey-puzzle' trees became common.

- **The huge, long-necked sauropods** of the Jurassic Period would have been able to reach high into tall conifer trees to rake off their needles.

- **In the Middle Cretaceous Period**, a new type of plant food appeared – the flowering plants.

- **By the end of the Cretaceous Period** there were many flowering trees and shrubs, such as magnolias, maples and walnuts.

- **No dinosaurs ate grass**, because grasses did not appear on Earth until 30–20 million years ago, long after the dinosaurs had died out.

> ...FASCINATING FACT...
> Gingkoes are still found today, in the form
> of maidenhair trees, with fan-shaped leaves.

Biggest

- **The biggest dinosaurs** were the sauropods such as *Brachiosaurus* and *Argentinosaurus* – but working out how heavy they were when they were alive is very difficult.

- *Brachiosaurus* **is known** from many remains, including almost complete skeletons, so its length can be measured accurately.

- **A dinosaur's weight** is estimated from a scaled-down model of its skeleton 'fleshed out' with muscles, guts and skin on the bones, using similar reptiles such as crocodiles for comparison.

- **The size of a dinosaur** model is measured by immersing it in water to find its volume.

- **The volume of a model dinosaur** is scaled up to find the volume of the real dinosaur when it was alive.

- **The sauropod** *Apatosaurus* is now well known from about 12 skeletons, which between them have almost every bone in its body.

- **Different experts** have 'fleshed out' the skeleton of *Apatosaurus* by different amounts, so estimates of its weight vary from 20 tonnes to more than 50 tonnes.

▲ *It is thought that despite its massive size,* Apatosaurus *would have been able to trot surprisingly quickly on its relatively long legs.*

> ... FASCINATING FACT ...
> The weights and volumes of reptiles alive today are used to calculate the probable weight of a dinosaur when it was alive.

A small mouth meant that a large sauropod like *Argentinosaurus* would have had to feed for about 20 hours each day!

Reconstruction of *Argentinosaurus* is based on relatively few of its bones, compared with other bones from similar sauropod dinosaurs

Argentinosaurus may have swallowed pebbles to help digest its food

Human-sized meat-eaters present little threat

Massive, heavy tail to swing at attackers

▲ Argentinosaurus *was a South American dinosaur, measuring up to 40 m long and weighing up to 100 tonnes. Despite this, fossil footprints show that some huge sauropods could run nearly as fast as a human!*

● **The length of** *Apatosaurus* is known accurately to have been 23 m.

● **Fossils of a dinosaur called** *Brontosaurus* were found to be identical to those of *Apatosaurus*, and since the name *Apatosaurus* had been given first, this was the name that had to be kept – so, officially, there is no dinosaur called *Brontosaurus*.

Sauropods

- **The sauropods** were the biggest of all the dinosaurs.

- **The huge plant-eating sauropods** lived mainly during the Jurassic Period, 208–144 million years ago.

- **A typical sauropod** had a tiny head, a very long neck and tail, a huge, bulging body and four massive legs, similar to those of an elephant, but much bigger.

- **Sauropods** included the well-known *Mamenchisaurus, Cetiosaurus, Diplodocus, Brachiosaurus* and *Apatosaurus*.

▼ Apatosaurus *was a huge sauropod, but it may have been able to rear up on its back legs in order to defend itself or its young.*

▼ *For many years, the longest dinosaur known from fairly complete fossil remains was the sauropod* Diplodocus. *However, other dinosaurs, known from fewer fossils, may have been longer. An almost complete fossil skeleton of* Diplodocus, *found around 1900, has been copied many times in plaster, plastic or glass fibre and sent to museums throughout the world.*

- *Rebbachisaurus* **fossils** were found in Morocco, Tunisia and Algeria.

- *Rebbachisaurus* **lived** 120 million years ago.

- *Cetiosaurus* was about 18 m long and weighed 30 tonnes.

- *Cetiosaurus*, **or 'whale reptile'**, was so-named because French fossil expert Georges Cuvier originally thought that its giant backbones came from a prehistoric whale.

- *Cetiosaurus* **was the first** sauropod to be given an official name, in 1841 – the year before the term 'dinosaur' was invented,

- **The first fossils** of *Cetiosaurus* were discovered in Oxfordshire, England, during the 1830s.

Brachiosaurus

- **Relatively complete** fossil remains exist of *Brachiosaurus*.

- *Brachiosaurus* was a sauropod – a huge plant-eater.

- **At 25 m long** from nose to tail, *Brachiosaurus* was one of the biggest of all dinosaurs.

- **Fossils** of *Brachiosaurus* have been found in North America, east and north Africa, and also possibly southern Europe.

- **Estimates of the weight** of *Brachiosaurus* range from about 30 to 75 tonnes.

- *Brachiosaurus* **lived** about 150 million years ago, and may have survived until 115 million years ago.

- **The name** *Brachiosaurus* means 'arm reptile' – it was so-named because of its massive front legs.

▼ Brachiosaurus *had similar body proportions to a giraffe, but was more than twice as tall and 50 times heavier.*

● **With its huge front legs** and long neck, *Brachiosaurus* could reach food more than 13 m from the ground.

● **The teeth** of *Brachiosaurus* were small and chisel-shaped for snipping leaves from trees.

● ***Brachiosaurus's*** nostrils were high on its head.

11

Diplodocus

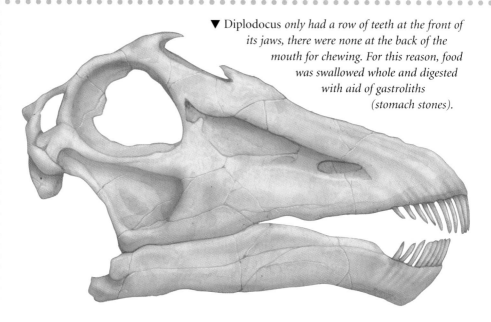

▼ Diplodocus *only had a row of teeth at the front of its jaws, there were none at the back of the mouth for chewing. For this reason, food was swallowed whole and digested with aid of gastroliths (stomach stones).*

- *Diplodocus* **was a huge plant-eating dinosaur** belonging to the group known as the sauropods.

- *Diplodocus* **lived** during the Late Jurassic Period, about 155–145 million years ago.

- **The first discovery** of *Diplodocus* fossils was in 1877, near Canyon City, Colorado, USA.

- **The main fossils** of *Diplodocus* were found in the Midwest of the USA, in Colorado, Utah and Wyoming.

- **At an incredible 27 m** or more in length, *Diplodocus* is one of the longest known dinosaurs.

- **Although so long,** *Diplodocus* was quite lightly built – it probably weighed 'only' 10–12 tonnes!

> ...**FASCINATING FACT**...
> *Diplodocus's* nostrils were so high on its skull that experts once thought it had a trunk!

- *Diplodocus* probably swung its tiny head on its enormous neck to reach fronds and foliage in the trees.

- **The teeth** of *Diplodocus* were slim rods that formed a comblike fringe only around the front of its mouth.

- *Diplodocus* **may have used** its comblike teeth to strip leaves from twigs and swallow them without chewing.

◄ Diplodocus was long but light for a sauropod, weighing 'only' about 10 tonnes. Like other sauropods, it used a combination of sheer size and a powerful whiplike tail to defend itself from predators.

13

Ankylosaurs

- **Ankylosaurs** had a protective armour of bony plates.

- **Unlike the armoured nodosaurs**, ankylosaurs had a large lump of bone at the ends of their tails, which they used as a hammer or club.

- **One of the best-known ankylosaurs**, from the preserved remains of about 40 individuals, is *Euoplocephalus*.

- ***Euoplocephalus*, or 'well-armoured head'**, had bony shields on its head and body, and even had bony eyelids. Blunt spikes ran along its back.

- **The hefty** *Euoplocephalus* was 7 m long and weighed 2 tonnes or more.

▲ *'Ankylosaur' means 'armoured reptile' and* Ankylosaurus *most certainly was. Even its skull was protected by bony plates although it had a soft, vulnerable belly which meant that it walked characteristically close to the ground.*

- *Euoplocephalus* lived about 75–70 million years ago in Alberta, Canada and Montana, USA.

- **Specimens of** *Euoplocephalus* are usually found singly, so it probably did not live in herds.

- **The ankylosaur** *Pinacosaurus* had bony nodules like chain-mail armour in its skin, and rows of blunt spikes from neck to tail.

- **Ankylosaurs** had small, weak teeth, and probably ate soft, low-growing ferns and horsetails.

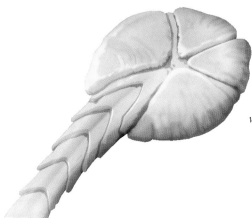

◀ *A powerful tail club was slow-moving* Ankylosaurus's *best weapon. It was made up of plates of fused bone and could be swung at an attacker with great force.*

Triceratops

▲ Triceratops *had a very short sturdy neck protected by a bony frill. In some ceratopsians however, the frill was simply very tough, bony skin which meant that it was a lot lighter.* Triceratops *moved in herds, giving it some protection from predators and was one of the last dinosaurs at the end of the Cretaceous Period.*

- **Many fossil remains** of *Triceratops* have been found. It is one of the most studied and best known dinosaurs.

- *Triceratops* **was the largest** of the plant-eating ceratopsians, the 'horn-faced' dinosaurs.

- *Triceratops* **lived at the very end** of the Age of Dinosaurs, about 67–65 million years ago.

- **Fossils of 50 or so** *Triceratops* have been found in North America, though no complete skeleton has been found.

- *Triceratops* **was about 9 m** long and weighed 5–6 tonnes – as big as the largest elephants of today.

- **As well as a short nose horn** and two long eyebrow horns, *Triceratops* also had a wide, sweeping frill that covered its neck like a curved plate.

- **The neck frill** of *Triceratops* may have been an anchor for the dinosaur's powerful chewing muscles.

- **Acting as a shield,** the bony neck frill of *Triceratops* may have protected it as it faced predators head-on.

- *Triceratops'* **neck frill** may have been brightly coloured, to impress rivals or warn off enemies.

- **The beaklike front** of *Triceratops'* mouth was toothless, but it had sharp teeth for chewing in its cheeks.

Heterodontosaurus

- **Heterodontosaurus was a very small dinosaur** at only 1.2 m in length (about as long as a large dog), and would have stood knee-high to a human.

- **Heterodontosaurus** lived about 205–195 million years ago, at the beginning of the Jurassic Period.

- **Probably standing partly upright** on its longer back legs, *Heterodontosaurus* would have been a fast runner.

- **Fossils** of *Heterodontosaurus* come from Lesotho in southern Africa and Cape Province in South Africa.

- **Most dinosaurs had teeth of only one shape** in their jaws, but *Heterodontosaurus* had three types of teeth.

▲ Heterodontosaurus *was a bipedal (two-legged), fast-moving, plant-eating dinosaur during the Early Jurassic Period (about 205 million years ago).*

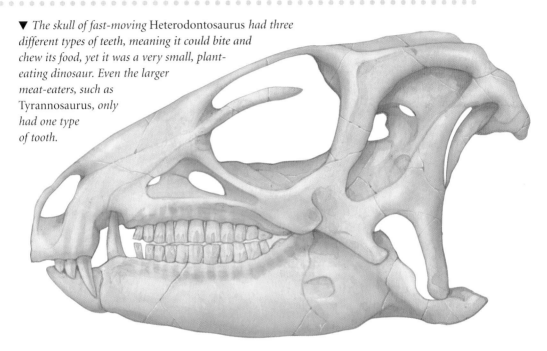

▼ *The skull of fast-moving* Heterodontosaurus *had three different types of teeth, meaning it could bite and chew its food, yet it was a very small, plant-eating dinosaur. Even the larger meat-eaters, such as* Tyrannosaurus, *only had one type of tooth.*

- **The front teeth** of *Heterodontosaurus* were small, sharp and found only in the upper jaw. They bit against the horny, beaklike lower front portion of the mouth.

- **The four middle teeth** of *Heterodontosaurus* were long and curved, similar to the tusks of a wild boar, and were perhaps used for fighting rivals or in self-defence.

- **The back or cheek teeth** of *Heterodontosaurus* were long and had sharp tops for chewing.

- *Heterodontosaurus* **probably ate** low-growing plants such as ferns.

19

Duck-bills

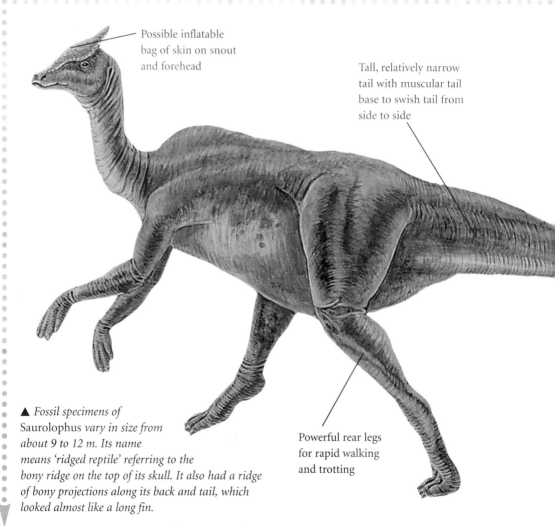

Possible inflatable bag of skin on snout and forehead

Tall, relatively narrow tail with muscular tail base to swish tail from side to side

Powerful rear legs for rapid walking and trotting

▲ *Fossil specimens of*
Saurolophus *vary in size from*
about 9 to 12 m. Its name
means 'ridged reptile' referring to the
bony ridge on the top of its skull. It also had a ridge
of bony projections along its back and tail, which
looked almost like a long fin.

- **'Duck-bills'** is the common name for the group of dinosaurs called the hadrosaurs.

- **Hadrosaurs were big plant-eaters** that walked mainly on their two large, powerful rear legs.

- **Hadrosaurs** were one of the last main dinosaur groups to appear on Earth, less than 100 million years ago.

- **Hadrosaurs were named after** *Hadrosaurus*, the first dinosaur of the group to be discovered as fossils, found in 1858 in New Jersey, USA.

- **Most hadrosaurs had wide mouths** that were flattened and toothless at the front, like a duck's beak.

- **Huge numbers of cheek teeth,** arranged in rows, filled the back of a hadrosaur's mouth. They were ideal for chewing tough plant food.

- **Some hadrosaurs** had tall, elaborate crests or projections of bone on their heads, notably *Corythosaurus*, *Tsintaosaurus*, *Saurolophus* and *Parasaurolophus*.

- **Hadrosaurs that lacked bony crests** and had low, smooth heads included *Anatosaurus*, *Bactrosaurus*, *Kritosaurus* and *Edmontosaurus*.

- **The name** *Hadrosaurus* means 'big reptile'.

> ### FASCINATING FACT
> *Edmontosaurus* may have had a loose bag of skin on its nose that it blew up like a balloon to make a honking or trumpeting noise – perhaps a breeding call.

Pachycephalosaurs

- **The pachycephalosaurs** are named after one of the best-known members of the group, *Pachycephalosaurus.*

- *Pachycephalosaurus* **means** 'thick-headed reptile', due to the domed and hugely thickened bone on the top of its skull – like a cyclist's crash helmet.

- **Pachycephalosaurs** were one of the last dinosaur groups to thrive. They lived 75–65 million years ago.

- **Pachycephalosaurs were plant-eaters** that stood up and ran on their longer back legs.

- *Pachycephalosaurus* was about 4.5 m long from nose to tail, and lived in the American Midwest.

- *Stegoceras*, also from the American Midwest, was 2.5 m long with a goat-sized body.

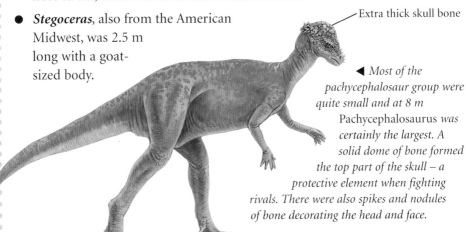

Extra thick skull bone

◀ *Most of the pachycephalosaur group were quite small and at 8 m* Pachycephalosaurus *was certainly the largest. A solid dome of bone formed the top part of the skull – a protective element when fighting rivals. There were also spikes and nodules of bone decorating the head and face.*

- *Homalocephale*, **another pachycephalosaur**, was about 3 m long and had a flatter skull. It lived in east Asia.

- **Pachycephalosaurs** may have defended themselves by lowering their heads and charging at their enemies.

- **At breeding time**, the males may have engaged in head-butting contests, as some sheep and goats do today.

▲ Stegoceras *was a bipedal (two-legged) dinosaur, but since it moved with its back level, it is unlikely to have been capable of great speed. However, the stance would be useful when involved in head-butting fights with rivals.*

Stegosaurs

- **Stegosaurs** were a group of plant-eating dinosaurs that lived mainly during the Late Jurassic Period, 160–140 million years ago.

> **...FASCINATING FACT...**
> The back plates of *Kentrosaurus* were leaf- or diamond-shaped to about halfway along its back, and spike-shaped on its hips and tail.

- **Stegosaurs are named after** the best-known of their group, *Stegosaurus*.

- **Stegosaurs are often called** 'plated dinosaurs', from the large, flat plates or slabs of bone on their backs.

- **Stegosaurs** probably first appeared in eastern Asia, then spread to other continents, especially North America and Africa.

▼ Kentrosaurus *had an unusual defensive display – a combination of plates and spikes running the length of the body and tail. The 'second brain' that was once thought to fill a space in a stegosaur's hip area is now known to have been a mass of nerves controlling the tail and back legs.*

24

▼ Stegosaurus *is thought to have had the smallest brain for its body size of all the dinosaurs, but the stegosaur group survived for more than 50 million years! It was a peaceful, slow-moving plant-eater, so did not need the brain power of a fast hunter like Troodon.*

- **The stegosaur** *Kentrosaurus* was about 5 m long and weighed an estimated 1 tonne.

- **The name** *Kentrosaurus* means 'spiky reptile'.

- ***Kentrosaurus*** lived about 155–150 million years ago in east Africa.

- **Most stegosaurs had no teeth** at the fronts of their mouths, but had horny beaks, like those of birds, for snipping off leaves.

- **Most stegosaurs chewed** their food with small, ridged cheek teeth.

Stegosaurus

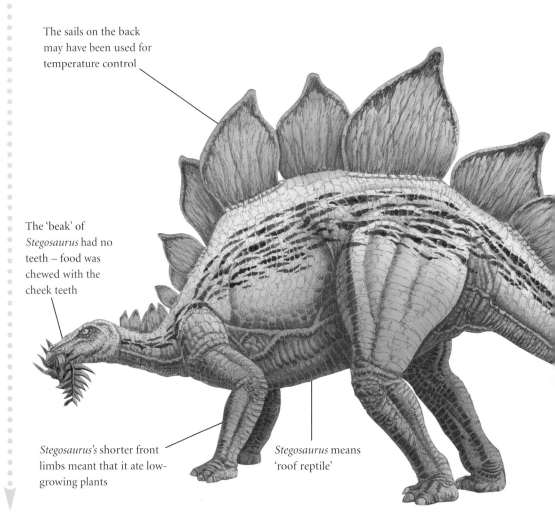

The sails on the back may have been used for temperature control

The 'beak' of *Stegosaurus* had no teeth – food was chewed with the cheek teeth

Stegosaurus's shorter front limbs meant that it ate low-growing plants

Stegosaurus means 'roof reptile'

- *Stegosaurus* was the largest of the stegosaur group.

- **Fossils of** *Stegosaurus* were found mainly in present-day Colorado, Utah and Wyoming, USA.

- *Stegosaurus,* **like most of its group**, lived towards the end of the Jurassic Period, about 150 million years ago.

- **The mighty** *Stegosaurus* was about 8–9 m long from nose to tail-tip and probably weighed more than 2 tonnes.

- **The most striking feature** of *Stegosaurus* was its large, roughly triangular bony plates along its back.

- **The name** *Stegosaurus* means 'roof reptile'. It was given this name because it was first thought that its 80-cm long bony plates lay flat on its back, overlapping slightly like the tiles on a roof.

- **It is now thought** that the back plates of *Stegosaurus* stood upright in two long rows.

- **The back plates** of *Stegosaurus* may have been for body temperature control, allowing the dinosaur to warm up quickly if it stood side-on to the sun's rays.

- *Stegosaurus's* **back plates** may have been covered with brightly coloured skin, possibly to intimidate enemies – they were too flimsy for protection.

- *Stegosaurus's* **tail** was armed with four large spikes, probably for swinging at enemies in self defence.

The spiked tail would have delivered a powerful blow

Ceratopsians

- **Ceratopsians** were large plant-eaters that appeared less than 90 million years ago.

- **Most ceratopsian fossils** come from North America.

- **'Ceratopsian' means 'horn-face',** after the long horns on their snouts, eyebrows or foreheads.

- **Most ceratopsians** had a neck shield or frill that swept sideways and up from behind the head to cover the upper neck and shoulders.

▼ *Chasmosaurus*

▼ *Triceratops*

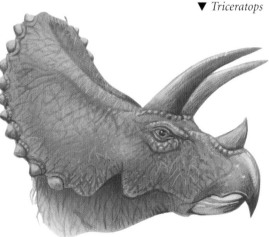

▶ Ceratopsians *were a group of dinosaurs with distinctive neck frills, horned faces and parrot-like beaks. They had very powerful jaws, allowing them to feed on tough plants. It is likely that they moved in herds. A mass grave of ceratopsians unearthed in Canada contained at least 300 skeletons.*

- **Well-known ceratopsians** included *Triceratops*, *Styracosaurus*, *Centrosaurus*, *Pentaceratops*, *Anchiceratops*, *Chasmosaurus* and *Torosaurus*.

- **The neck frills of some ceratopsians**, such as that of *Chasmosaurus*, had large gaps or 'windows' in the bone.

- **In life**, the windows in the neck frill of a ceratopsian were covered with thick, scaly skin.

- **Ceratopsians** had no teeth in the fronts of their hooked, beaklike mouths.

- **Using rows of powerful cheek teeth**, ceratopsians sheared their plant food.

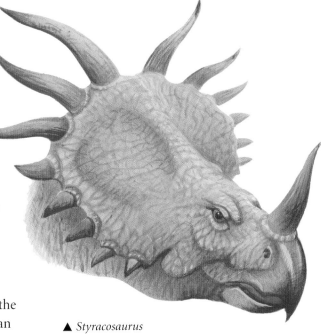

▲ *Styracosaurus*

FASCINATING FACT
Torosaurus had the longest skull of any land animal ever, at 2.5 m from the front of the snout to the rear of the neck frill.

Tuojiangosaurus

- *Tuojiangosaurus* was a member of the group we know as the plated dinosaurs, or stegosaurs.

- **The first nearly complete dinosaur skeleton** to be found in China was of a *Tuojiangosaurus*, and excellent fossil skeletons are on display in several Chinese museums.

- **The name** *Tuojiangosaurus* means 'Tuo River reptile'.

- *Tuojiangosaurus* lived during the Late Jurassic Period, about 155 million years ago.

- *Tuojiangosaurus* was 7 m long from nose to tail-tip.

- **The weight of** *Tuojiangosaurus* was probably about one tonne.

- **Like other stegosaurs**, *Tuojiangosaurus* had tall slabs or plates of bone on its back.

- **The back plates of** *Tuojiangosaurus* were roughly triangular and probably stood upright in two rows that ran from the neck to the middle of the tail.

- *Tuojiangosaurus* **plucked low-growing plant food** with the beak-shaped front of its mouth, and partly chewed the plant material with its leaf-shaped, ridge-edged cheek teeth.

▶ Tuojiangosaurus *was a stegosaur, a group of heavily armoured, small-brained herbivores that survived for over 50 million years. Stegosaurs' main defence was their tail. It could deliver a powerful blow with cone-shaped plates on the underside and long wounding spikes at the end.*

FASCINATING FACT

Tuojiangosaurus had four long tail spikes,
arranged in two Vs, which it could swing
at enemies to keep them at a distance.

Iguanodon

- *Iguanodon* **was a large plant-eater** in the dinosaur group known as ornithopods.

- **Numerous fossils** of *Iguanodon* have been found in several countries in Europe, including England, Belgium, Germany and Spain.

- *Iguanodon* measured about 9 m from nose to tail.

- **A large elephant today**, at 4–5 tonnes, is estimated to weigh about the same as *Iguanodon* did.

- *Iguanodon* **lived** during the Early to Middle Cretaceous Period, 140–110 million years ago.

- *Iguanodon* **probably walked** and ran on its large, powerful back legs for much of the time, with its body held horizontal.

▲ *When a fossil of the thumb spike was first unearthed, palaeontologists thought it belonged on* Iguanodon's *nose!*

32

▶ *Herbivorous* Iguanodon *may have used its large thumb spike as defence against enemies. It would have delivered a nasty stab wound to the neck or flank.*

- **A cone-shaped spike** on *Iguanodon*'s thumb may have been a weapon for jabbing at rivals or enemies.

- **The three central fingers** on *Iguanodon*'s hands had hooflike claws for four-legged walking.

- **The fifth or little finger** of *Iguanodon* was able to bend across the hand for grasping objects, and was perhaps used to pull plants towards the mouth.

◀ Iguanodon *had claws on its feet. But these were rounded and blunt and looked more like hooves.*

33

Nodosaurs

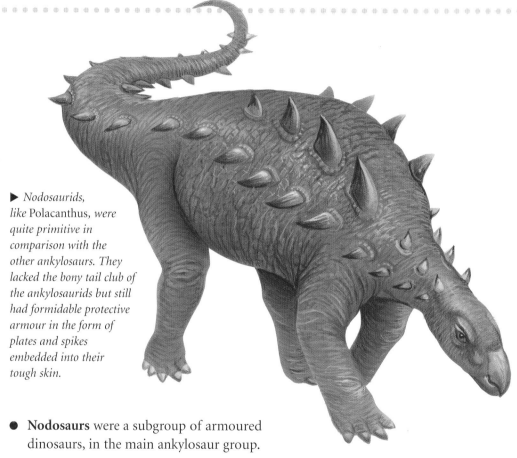

▶ *Nodosaurids, like* Polacanthus, *were quite primitive in comparison with the other ankylosaurs. They lacked the bony tail club of the ankylosaurids but still had formidable protective armour in the form of plates and spikes embedded into their tough skin.*

- **Nodosaurs** were a subgroup of armoured dinosaurs, in the main ankylosaur group.

- **The nodosaur subgroup** included *Edmontonia, Sauropelta, Polacanthus* and *Nodosaurus*.

- **Nodosaurs were slow-moving**, heavy-bodied plant-eaters with thick, heavy nodules, lumps and plates of bone in their skin for protection.

- **Most nodosaurs lived** during the Late Jurassic and the Cretaceous Periods, 150–65 million years ago.

- *Edmontonia* **lived in North America** during the Late Cretaceous Period, 75–70 million years ago.

- *Edmontonia* **was about seven metres long**, but its bony armour made it very heavy for its size, at 4–5 tonnes.

- **Along its neck, back and tail** *Edmontonia* had rows of flat and spiky plates.

- **The nodosaur** *Polacanthus* was about 4 m long and lived 120–110 million years ago.

- **Fossils** of *Polacanthus* come from the Isle of Wight, southern England, and perhaps from North America, in South Dakota, USA.

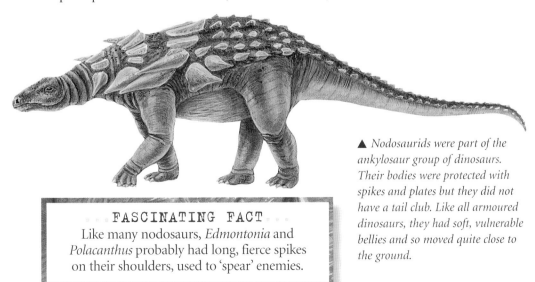

▲ *Nodosaurids were part of the ankylosaur group of dinosaurs. Their bodies were protected with spikes and plates but they did not have a tail club. Like all armoured dinosaurs, they had soft, vulnerable bellies and so moved quite close to the ground.*

FASCINATING FACT
Like many nodosaurs, *Edmontonia* and *Polacanthus* probably had long, fierce spikes on their shoulders, used to 'spear' enemies.

Segnosaurs

- **Little is known** about the segnosaur group of dinosaurs – the subject of much disagreement among experts.

- **Segnosaurs are named after** almost the only known member of the group, Segnosaurus.

▼ Segnosaurus *is one of those dinosaurs that we just don't know that much about. Scientists have grouped it with the sauropods, but it has some unusual additional features! Instead of having four stocky legs, it may have moved around quite easily on two legs, using its clawed front feet to feed. We do know that it ate plants, but it may have eaten meat as well which no other sauropod did.*

▶ *Another unusual feature of* Segnosaurus *was that it was not typically lizard-hipped.*

- **The name Segnosaurus** means 'slow reptile'.

- **Segnosaurus lived** during the Mid to Late Cretaceous Period, about 90 million years ago.

- **Fossils of Segnosaurus** were found mainly in the Gobi Desert in Central Asia in the 1970s. The dinosaur was named in 1979 by Mongolian scientist Altangerel Perle.

- **Segnosaurus had a narrow head** and probably a toothless, beaklike front to its mouth.

- **Experts** have variously described Segnosaurus as a predatory meat-eater, a swimming or wading fish-eater, a rearing-up leaf-eater, or even an ant-eater.

- **Different experts** have said Segnosaurus was a theropod, a prosauropod and an ornithopod.

- **Some scientists have suggested** that Segnosaurus was a huge dinosaur-version of today's anteater that ripped open the nests of termites and ants with its powerful claws.

Sauropelta

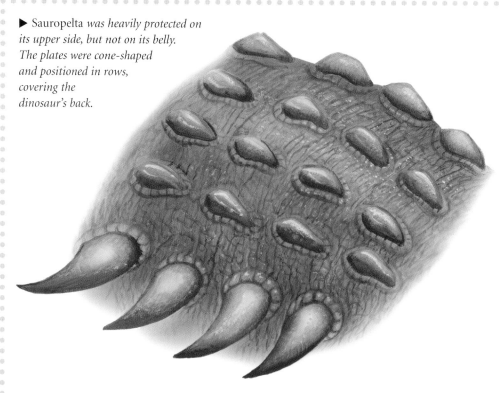

▶ Sauropelta *was heavily protected on its upper side, but not on its belly. The plates were cone-shaped and positioned in rows, covering the dinosaur's back.*

- ***Sauropelta*** was a nodosaur – a type of armoured dinosaur.

- **The name** *Sauropelta* means 'shielded reptile', from the many large, conelike lumps of bone – some almost as big as dinner plates – on its head, neck, back and tail.

- **The larger lumps of bone** on *Sauropelta* were interspersed with smaller, fist-sized bony studs.

Sauropelta lived 110–100 million years ago,
in present-day Montana and Wyoming, USA.

- *Sauropelta* **had a row of sharp spikes** along each side of its body, from just behind the eyes to the tail. The spikes decreased in size towards the tail.

- *Sauropelta* **was about 7.5 m long**, including the tail, and its bulky body and heavy, bony armour meant it probably weighed almost 3 tonnes.

- **The armour** of *Sauropelta* was flexible, almost like lumps of metal set into thick leather, so the dinosaur could twist and turn, but was unable to run very fast.

- **Strong, sturdy, pillar-like legs** supported *Sauropelta's* great weight.

- *Sauropelta* probably defended itself by crouching down to protect its softer belly, or swinging its head to jab at an enemy with its long neck spines.

- **Using its beak-like mouth**, *Sauropelta* probably plucked at low-growing plant food.

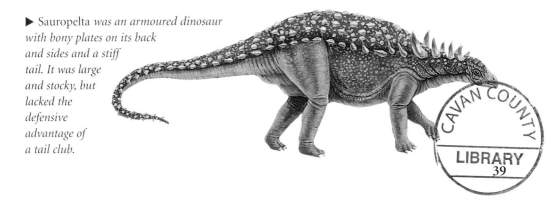

▶ Sauropelta *was an armoured dinosaur with bony plates on its back and sides and a stiff tail. It was large and stocky, but lacked the defensive advantage of a tail club.*

Index